Waking Oz

Sue Tabb & Deirdre Budzyna

A Guide for Women Who Want to Use Brains, Heart, and Courage to Create a Kickass Life

Copyright © 2024 Sue Tabb and Deirdre Budzyna

All rights reserved.

This is a work of fiction. Names, characters, places, and incidents are either a product of the author's imagination or are used fictitiously, and any resemblance to actual persons, living or dead, business establishments, events, or locales is entirely coincidental. No part of this book may be reproduced or transmitted in any form or by any means, graphic, electronic, or mechanical, including photocopying recording, or taping without the written consent of the author or publisher.

Briley & Baxter Publications | Plymouth, Massachusetts

ISBN: 978-1-961978-42-3

Book Design: Amy Deyerle-Smith

To Sue and Shirley: Two mothers who always encourage us to click our heels and jump into the twister. Thank you for showing us the path to Oz is all about the journey.

We love you!

CONTENTS

1	INTRODUCTION
5	COME OUT, COME OUT WHEREVER YOU ARE
11	ON PLAYING PERFECT
19	WHO ARE YOU AGAIN?
23	HOW THE HELL DID I GET *HERE?*
31	IT'S NEVER TOO LATE FOR A DO-OVER
37	WANT TO PLAY WITH A LITTLE FIRE?
43	ON FALLING DOWN SPECTACULARLY
49	WOMEN WHO ARE CLICKING
53	SAYING IT OUT LOUD
57	KICK UP A TWISTER, SISTER!
75	NOW, RELEASE THE FLYING MONKEYS!

"We are all busy, but having a busy life is different than having a full life. A full life is harder to achieve but immeasurably more satisfying."

INTRODUCTION

Oz is an interesting place. You see it from afar and it's a glistening, magical land where wishes are granted and dreams come true. And what's better, there's a yellow brick road to take you there. At some point in our lives, we've all bought into the fantasy that somewhere, somehow, there is that perfect place where beauty, happiness, and success all intersect at once; an Oz-like utopia that will appear in the distance if we wish hard enough. But the truth is Oz doesn't exist. At least not in the way Dorothy imagined it. It's a bullshit concept, an illusion surrounded by the misconception that our destiny is rolled out in front of us like a well-laid brick road. But there is no road, there are no bricks, and there definitely is no Great and Powerful Oz. Never has been.

Oz is more a state of mind; a place of power; a feeling of fulfillment. And what Oz looks like for you is definitely not what it looks like for someone else. Everyone has their own unique version. The problem is that many of us, particularly women, have forgotten what it looks like or how to use our power to get there.

This book is a first step in waking the power of Oz. **YOUR OZ.**

Here's the situation: You wake up one day to find crow's feet, a kid with a license, and a stalling career. You are driving a car you hate, your nails are mangled stubs, and you are wearing those comfortable shoes that, let's be honest, don't flatter anyone. What happened? Time goes by gradually but the realization of your current lot hits you in the face like a frying pan—a cast iron one. Many of us have made the ultimate sacrifice: We put our family first—particularly our kids—at the expense of ourselves. We've forgotten that it's an equal opportunity organization and that our needs are just as important as every other member's needs. We've elevated ourselves to the master of everyone's destiny except our own. We need to get over ourselves. Because here's the cold, hard truth:

Your kids don't need you as much as you think.

Too many of us hide behind our kids and make their lives *our* lives. It's just too much for both parties. There have been dozens of books written about the harm we do to our kids—stifling their independence, not allowing them to develop problem-solving skills—but very few deal with what this style of parenting is doing to the parents themselves, particularly the mothers.

There has been a hefty price to pay. Lots of mothers we interviewed shared the toll this method of parenting has taken on them. Many feel lost, dispassionate, or even depressed. Many feel like they've lost their power and don't know where to begin to take it back. And some don't even know what "it" is anymore.

This book intends to help women find their way back to their core.

We believe it's time to wake up and make some changes. As women, many of us have been hiding from our truth—we're getting older, which means our kids will leave and we darn well better have a life carved out for ourselves.

We've gone overboard making it all about our kids. So, it's time to step out because there really is no wizard behind the green curtain to magically take care of everything. Remember what Glinda said? "You always had the power my dear; you just had to learn it for yourself."

Let's begin with the magic slippers. Look down; you are wearing them. They look different on each of us. Some of us are wearing heels, some are wearing flats and some are wearing those "comfortable" shoes. The point is we all have shoes and those shoes hold our power. You can walk in them, run in them, or kick some serious ass in them.

So, the question is: What are you doing in *your* shoes?

Have you forgotten how to click your heels? It's never too late. It doesn't matter if you are thirty, forty, fifty, or eighty, your shoes still work; dust them off and use them.

This book is a wake-up call and a road map. Stop imagining there is a yellow brick road waiting for you. Your road might have purple stones or red gravel or green dirt, but it's your road to build and travel. When are you going to start? The road is where you gather rich experiences and friendships that support your efforts to create your version of the Emerald City.

Remember, your spouse can't find it for you; your kids can't find it for you; only you can find it. There is no one on the planet who wants exactly the same thing.

Brains, heart and courage will get you there. Yup, it turns out we can learn a lot from *The Wizard of Oz*.

You need to exercise your mind, find your passion, and take some risks. But like Dorothy, many of us forget we have the power to do it. Other things get in the way—like managing the everyday stuff. We lose our way and forget that our journey is important. We are all busy, but having a busy life is different than having a full life. A full life is harder to achieve but immeasurably more satisfying.

We hope our advice and collective experience will make you laugh, will inspire you, and will force you to be honest with yourself and commit to making a change. It takes a lot of courage to live a life that reflects who you are and honors your skills. But it will take even more courage to face a life of regrets. And you don't have to map the human genome or win the Nobel Peace Prize. Not having regrets simply means honoring your own potential. The time is now to click your heels and watch the magic happen.

It's time to jump into the twister, sister. We are with you.

"One day you look in the mirror and wonder where all the years went, and who the person looking back at you really is. We've been hiding behind our kids for too long. It's time to step out from behind the curtain."

chapter one

COME OUT, COME OUT WHEREVER YOU ARE

Or: Get over yourself—your children don't need you as much as you think.

Stop gasping. We know this kind of thinking is counterculture to everything we have been living these past years. If we are "good" parents then our kids must be the center of our universe, our number one priority, and, in fact, most of us have altered our lives to accommodate their needs and wants. So, we've been good parents. Heck, we've been better than good. We've made it all about our kids. And while our kids might say it's been just fine, thank you, we'd like to suggest that there is a problem.

When we make it ALL about the kids, we sell ourselves short. And we don't notice it right away—sometimes for years—but it eventually catches up with us. One day you look in the mirror and wonder where all the years went, and who the person looking back at you really is. We've been hiding behind our kids for too long. It's time to step out from behind the curtain.

We know what some of you are thinking: Wait, I chose this! Yes, but that doesn't mean that "this" is all there is. You are a multi-dimensional person who is defined by more than just parenthood. And it doesn't matter if you work part-time, full-time, don't work, or work two jobs. This isn't about how much you work or how much money you make. It's about making a life and pursuing interests that honor who you are. Just you.

Here's a news flash: *You are as important as anyone in your family.* No one comes first. We know you love your partner and your children, but they don't need you to control every aspect of their lives. In fact, please stop.

Here's the thing: we've done it too. We act like martyrs and then wonder why people treat us as though our needs are less important. We created a situation that invites people to do so.

Does this sound like a typical morning in your house? You wake up, put on the coffee, load the dishwasher, feed the dogs, throw in a load of laundry, make breakfast, pack lunches, check email, kiss everyone on their way out the door and then realize you've been up for an hour and haven't even had a chance to go to the bathroom?

How about the end of the day? It's more of the same. You meant to go to that yoga class, meet the girls for a drink, or read the last chapter of that book, but there just isn't enough time in the day. There isn't time because we don't make ourselves a priority. This is the mindset that must change. You have to make time for your own life because, in the end, that is the only constant you have. Kids leave, marriages can break up, times change. You need to have the ability to react to those changes by drawing on the resources and the life you've created for yourself.

It has occurred to more than one of us that we are getting a raw deal. Not only do we have the older model cell phone, the second job and the "on-call" shuttle driver status, we have kids who are not necessarily benefitting from our behavior. Perhaps, just perhaps, our kids don't really need us as much as we think.

Yes, we went ahead and said the unthinkable. Our kids need us, sure. We need to be there to teach them right from wrong and to dust them off when they fall and guide them through life's tricky twists and turns. But many of us are taking it so much farther than that. We are bubble-wrapping a generation of kids in an effort to protect them from life's harsh realities.

It all comes from a place of love, but we are misplacing our focus. We have forgotten that giving our kids every creature comfort, solving their every problem, and being available to them 24/7 isn't necessarily being the best parent. It sure looks good on the surface, but we're doing them and ourselves a disservice. We are robbing them of important life experiences and robbing ourselves of our own life experiences.

Many of us are trying to live life *for* our kids. They frankly don't want that. We have an inflated sense of our importance as they grow. We need to get over ourselves a bit here. Seriously. Our kids don't really want us as involved as we are. We have managed to convince ourselves that our hyper-attentiveness is a barometer for good parenting. But it's time to take a step back. Let's start by discussing why it's not good for our kids. We'll move on to you in a moment. (This really is all about you).

In a 2015 interview with NPR, Jessica Lahey, the author of *The Gift of Failure: How the Best Parents Learn to Let Go So Their Children Can Succeed* said this: "After three years of research and a lot of soul-searching, here's where I've ended up: Kids are anxious, afraid and risk-averse because parents are more focused on keeping their children safe, content, and happy in the moment than on parenting for competence."

We are stripping our kids of opportunities for growth by solving their problems, encouraging safety and comfort over risk, and limiting their ability to develop resiliency by protecting them from necessary challenges and disappointments.

How often as parents do we assemble the science fair dioramas, call the teacher to explain why Johnny should be excused for not handing in his homework, solve an argument Susie had with a friend by calling the friend's mom, give AJ our phone when he lost his, or buy a present for a sibling on their sister's birthday so they won't feel bad? Does any of this sound familiar?

In that same interview we heard some great advice by the author of the book *How to Raise an Adult: Break Free of the Overparenting Trap and Prepare Your Kid for Success*. Julie Lythcott-Haims says she fell victim to overparenting after realizing that, despite being a college dean discouraging parents for being too involved in their students' lives, she was cutting the meat of her eight- and ten-year-old kids.

Let's be honest with ourselves; most of us are guilty of at least one of these so-called infractions. And what occurred to us is that *our* parents were not doing any of the above. They were not disinterested or unsupportive, to the contrary, they understood how to be separate but supportive. They didn't live *for* us, they lived alongside us, with us.

Ask yourself this question: Who are you living for, really? By living for our kids, we are failing ourselves.

> "The greatest harm to a child is the unlived life of the parent."
> ~ Carl Jung

At the end of the day, you have to make time for your own life because that is the only constant you have. We realize this isn't easy. Many of us are juggling a job, family, volunteer work, and outside responsibilities. Making yourself a priority means making some changes because no one can do it all.

Try this: Right now, describe yourself using three words NOT in relation to anyone else. Don't use words like mom, wife, friend, or nurturer. Use words to describe your specific skill set, passions, or talents. Define YOU.

Ready, set, go:

1.

2.

3.

When we do this exercise in our workshops, our participants struggle. It's not easy to unveil yourself and look at who you are when you strip away who you are to other people. But enough is enough. It's time to give yourself permission to pursue your own dreams and to carve out a life that honors your passions and skills. Remember: it's *your* road, *your* Oz, *your* Emerald City.

Mothers struggle a great deal with this concept because we have a natural tendency to surrender the ship as soon as the baby tug arrives. The problem is that the ship still needs to be fueled, directed, and ultimately brought to shore. Choose YOU.

As we move into the next chapter, ponder this question:

Would you rather captain the ship or go down a martyr?

Answer these questions honestly:

* When was the last time you reached a personal goal?
* How many chapters of YOUR book center solely on your kids?
* Remember the aspirations you had in your early twenties? Are there any that are still brewing under the surface?

Write about one thing you can do (independent of your kids or spouse) to make yourself a priority:

_____

"Many of us spend our days negotiating a brutal set of demands, a harried schedule and the financial strain of keeping up with our contemporaries. We are often fooling ourselves by 'playing perfect' and measuring ourselves against an impossible standard."

chapter two
ON PLAYING PERFECT

Or: Have the courage to show the cracks in your armor.

Today's world is more complex than the world our parents and grandparents lived in. It is a vastly different culture from even the time when these authors grew up, with the onslaught of high-tech products that provide ease and efficiency but also constant access and exposure. Whether this environment is better or worse is a debate for another book; our point is that it is here, and with it comes challenges that have very capable people feeling, at times, vulnerable and out of control. Many of us spend our days negotiating a brutal set of demands, a harried schedule, and the financial strain of keeping up with our contemporaries. We are often fooling ourselves by "playing perfect" and measuring ourselves against an impossible standard. There has been a price to pay.

Many of us believe that no one else can make the bed like us, unload the dishwasher like us, or grocery shop like us. But that is simply not true. We may like the control, but in the end, we are not the best ones for the job every time. And if you absorb yourself into serving others' needs 24/7, you WILL lose yourself.

It's just not possible to have a spotless house, a perfect marriage, flawless children, your dream job, and well-sculpted abs. (The abs might be the hardest part here.) The point is that many of us pretend we've got it all in balance. We want to be like the families around us who seem to have it all figured out. But you will exhaust yourself trying to keep up with the Joneses. No one's life is exactly as it appears. No one has it all. Someone will always appear to have more than you, but you don't know their truth.

Concentrate on what you have. Make the most of your own life. And just cut yourself a little slack once in a while.

Actor Kristen Bell made some very insightful comments in the October 2017 issue of *Redbook* regarding being real with others: "Humans want nothing more than to be accepted, and I'm no different. That doesn't happen by presenting perfection. I believe in showing your dirty hands and your bumps and bruises and your faults, because that's what makes people feel connected—and isn't that kind of the purpose of, you know, being on Earth?"

In the same article she reminded all of us that we have no idea what someone else is going through, quoting wisdom her mom passed down: "Just because you don't see the chinks in a person's armor doesn't mean you can treat them like you know their story." Bell went on to question the concept of balance, saying balance is not stationary but rather moves like a teeter totter. There is always give and take. Everyone is just trying to do their best.

Yes! We couldn't agree more, but let's all tell the truth about where we are on the teeter totter. We need to be real with one another, ask for help, and connect with others because we all struggle with the demands of life. We need to stop pretending we have it all in balance all of the time. Absolutely NO ONE does. And we'll all be a lot happier if we accept our imperfect truth. There's a freedom in showing the cracks in your armor and it certainly relieves the pressure of appearing perfect.

What is clear is that many people, particularly women, needlessly suffer in silence. When others come forward and open up about their struggles, we slowly come to understand that this journey is traveled by many intelligent people. We have the utmost respect for those who have talked about their shortcomings publicly, since they have the courage to acknowledge their humanness. It's time we not only show, but embrace, our imperfectness. We are human and we need to let go of the unrealistic ideal we have adopted. It is unattainable. Period. Let it go and be open. This will give others permission to do so as well. We take ourselves way too seriously.

Guess what?

It's okay to miss your kid's soccer or lacrosse game occasionally.

It's okay to pick up food at a drive-through when you've had the day from Hell.

It's okay to walk the 5k your friends may be running.

It's okay to have dinner with a friend instead of being "on call" at home.

It's okay to limit Johnny to one extracurricular activity so you can take that art class.

It's okay to leave your kids with a sitter once a week so you can have a date night with your partner.

It's okay to go on vacation without your kids.

This column, written by co-author Sue Tabb, demonstrates the imperfectness we have to learn to accept and even embrace as parents:

A Kernel of Truth

I am not a great cook. I am not even a pretty good cook. I am the type of cook who prepares a meal because eating is a requirement to stay alive. Based on that motivation, you can imagine the zest with which I approach dinner preparation. Yup, it's like watching a twelve-year-old do his algebra homework...without a pencil, a calculator, or the will to live.

Every day it's the same thing: six o'clock rolls around and I wonder what gourmet creation I can whip up in seven minutes or, and this is always my preference, if I can get away with a frozen pizza for the third night in a row. I have come to loathe this time of day, and for no reason other than having to come up with something my family members can push around on their plates while telling me how much they dislike it. Thankfully, they are always subtle and respectful when sharing their mutual disgust. (i.e. What is that nasty thing? What is this supposed to taste like? Is this burnt or just gross?)

Anyway, I'm only sharing my lack of culinary talent as a preface to a story about an experience at my daughter's school that has forced me to take a hard look at the facts. First of all, I need to take a cooking class. Secondly, I need to read my emails a bit more carefully. Thirdly, I need to come to grips with the painful reality that my daughter's teachers will never again ask for an edible contribution from my household without express written instruction. No, not even then.

It all began simply enough. After finishing a unit on the Iroquois Indians, my daughter's class was going to hold a celebration honoring their traditions to include Indian-inspired food, dance and craft making. As parents, we were instructed to contribute by helping our children prepare a dish to share at the celebration. The key phrase here is "prepare a dish," which I apparently glazed over during the initial reading of the e-mail instructions.

My daughter came home one day and announced that she had signed up for corn. I asked the obvious questions: What kind of corn? How much? Canned or frozen? To each of my inquiries she looked stumped but then shrugged it off, telling me that a can of corn was fine. She did make one request, to dump it into a Tupperware bowl. Okay, even I—the anti-Rachel Ray—could handle that. Or so I thought.

I didn't remember my commitment until ten p.m. the evening before. Of course, I was out of canned corn and none of my neighbors, who have things like cilantro and organic lemonade in their kitchens, had a single kernel. I ran to the local supermarket the next morning, picked up two cans of corn, and hand-delivered them to the school. I was proud of myself because, as instructed, I placed the corn—still in the pop-top cans—into a Tupperware dish so that it was ready for the microwave. I even picked up some extra cornbread in case they ran out. How very thoughtful of me.

Then the other mothers pulled up to the school and ruined everything. As I stood proudly with my Market Basket bag, they pulled pots and dishes of homemade treats out of their cars. One mother had risen from bed at five a.m. to make the cornbread from scratch; the other had made turkey soup. I was half expecting someone to arrive with a breaded cornucopia. And there I stood with my canned corn.

These were the good mothers of the world. And, although their domestic prowess made me look like a complete failure, they were kind enough to support my imperfect contribution and even applauded my last-minute resourcefulness. You see why it's impossible for me to dislike these women.

My offering was certainly appreciated, and I heard (from a little Iroquois birdie) that my store-bought cornbread was gobbled up. However, I think we missed the point of the exercise. Or perhaps I was behind a unit since they had recently studied food groups and how products arrive on supermarket shelves. I would have been better suited for that one.

The good news is that my daughter was happy to see me when I arrived and wasn't at all embarrassed by my less-than-stellar presentation. I figure she understands my limitations at this point and simply appreciates the effort. And it's really all I can ask for since she's eaten a lot of microwaved canned corn in the past 10 years. Not that there's anything wrong with that.

The point is to live in a way that more fairly reflects your current circumstances and your own personal needs because there is a real danger in playing perfect. It can often lead to anxiety and, in some cases, depression. Identifying the specific triggers that can lead to a depressive episode is not yet an exact science. There is a plethora of research that points to chemical imbalances, neurological problems, and hormonal changes. And while many experts believe that there are significant physiological indicators, there is no way to ignore the situational and societal factors that can play a significant role. Trying to pretend you lead the perfect life can only increase a person's likelihood of developing an anxiety-related disorder.

You need to live your truth.

These authors will openly admit it is not always easy to live in a way that reflects your values and priorities. We are not always successful and jealousy can still rear its ugly head from time to time. However, we have (albeit slowly) come to accept the fact that there will always be people who *appear* to have it all no matter what we've managed to accomplish. Here's the truth:
Someone will always have a nicer home.
Someone will always drive a more expensive car.
Someone will always take fancier vacations.
Someone will always have a more glamorous job.
Someone will always appear to be living that enviable, perfect life.
Once you accept this sobering reality, you can focus less on others and simply deal with your own situation. What will define a good life for you? Everyone's list will be different because everyone has their own priorities and their own ideas about the kind of life they want to create. You need to understand that comparing yourself with someone who has a different set of dreams and financial resources will only serve to drain your energy and,

even worse, create conditions that can breed depression and/or anxiety.

You are not alone. According to the National Institute of Mental Health (NIMH), anxiety disorders are the most common mental illness in the U.S., affecting nineteen percent of adults, with a higher prevalence in women than in men (twenty-three percent versus fourteen percent). From puberty to age fifty, women are nearly twice as likely as men to be diagnosed with an anxiety disorder according to the Anxiety and Depression Association of America. And while anxiety disorders are highly treatable, only thirty-seven percent of US adults receive treatment.

These statistics are not only startling but a good reminder to look around. You probably know several women—some even in your inner circle of friends—who are suffering right now. Many suffer in silence because they are embarrassed to talk about it, admit they need help, or are unable to get the care they need. Despite the cause of your specific episode, it has been our experience in talking with so many people who have suffered that there are remarkable similarities in the way that we feel, the way that we perceive the world, and the way we approach recovery. Talking about the experience, sharing stories, and yes, even laughing about some of our misconceptions and irrational worries, can help us feel less isolated and more in control. The one thread absolutely consistent throughout our discussions was the sentiment that *maybe I am going crazy*. You are not going crazy. If you have the wherewithal to read this book, you are likely a sane and capable person going through a transitional time.

And there is no shame in getting help. Engaging the help of a therapist is not an admission that you are any less sane than you were prior to feeling symptomatic. Most people who see a therapist—and there are millions of them—are very high-functioning people. It's never a bad idea to have an objective professional help you work through life's ongoing struggles.

A good therapist will act as your mirror—sometimes providing you with a way to really see yourself for the first time. Your husband, mother, or best friend may have told you a hundred times that you have trouble setting limits, or saying no, or taking time for yourself. When the therapist tells you, you are free of distractions and the emotions tied to the communicator; the message can be heard and processed at a different level. It is communication at its purest form. In today's society, where we are bombarded with so many forms of one-dimensional piecemeal communications, it is valuable to receive this type of feedback.

"There's no need to be perfect to inspire others. Let people get inspired by how you deal with your imperfections."
-Ziad K. Abdelnour

Here is today's challenge: STOP PLAYING PERFECT! If you let go of perfection you will have time to do things that spark your creativity, speak to your heart, and make you think critically. Encourage the women in your life to feel safe to do the same. Share your goals, your shortcomings, your innermost fears, and your successes. Allow yourself the freedom to celebrate your imperfectness. This will allow you to move forward into discovery mode. It will free you up to take risks, chase dreams, and learn new things. It is truly the best gift you could give yourself. Consider this: In Japan, broken objects are often repaired with gold. The flaw is seen as a unique piece of the object's history, which adds to its beauty.

So, as we move into the next chapter, ponder this question:

Would you rather be a shiny bowl with no history or a cracked bowl with lots of stories to tell?

Answer these questions honestly:

* What defines a "good" life for you?

* When do you find yourself playing perfect? Who does it benefit?

* What is one thing you can let go of to make time for something that truly speaks to your heart?

"Don't wait until the kids are gone to start nurturing the marriage; if you haven't put in the time and energy before that, it could be too late."

chapter three

WHO ARE YOU AGAIN?

Or: How brains, heart and courage keep you interesting to your partner.

A person who is achieving their goals, chasing their dreams, and doing things that speak to their values is far more attractive to their partner. Your partner will respect your drive and your desire to fulfill your potential. Please stop saying "My kids come first." No one should come first. All family members are equal. Kids should see that your marriage is as important as your role as a parent. Make time for that relationship.Here's something to think about: we have unconditional love for our kids. There is virtually no situation in which we can imagine not loving them. Even if they behave badly, we forgive and hope they learn from their mistakes. Hell, they can lie, cheat, even steal and we will still love them. We wouldn't like or condone that behavior—we would be extremely disappointed—but our love is unwavering. Not so for our partners. Most of us have conditions on that relationship. There is no cheating allowed. We demand respect. We demand trust and transparency. We want an equal partnership with mutual admiration for one another. But that takes WAY more work. So that relationship has to be, at a minimum, as important as your relationship with your kids. If you ignore it, there is a price to pay later.

Don't wait until the kids are gone to start nurturing the marriage; if you haven't put in the time and energy before that, it will be too late. In a 2014 article by physician and researcher Danielle Teller titled "How American Parenting is Killing the American Marriage," Teller wrote, "Children who are raised to believe that they are the center of the universe have a tough time when their special status erodes as they approach adulthood. Most troubling of all, couples who live entirely child-centric lives can lose touch with one another to the point where they have nothing left to say to one another when the kids leave home."

In the 21st century, we marry for love. Most of us believe our partners will be our soulmates for life. When children come along, we often shift our focus and become solely dedicated to their growth and well-being. Our partners can suffer. It is difficult to press "pause" on a relationship for eighteen or twenty years and expect to pick up where you left off. According to Pew Research, divorce rates are climbing for empty nesters. At a time when divorce is becoming less common for younger adults, so-called "gray divorce" is on the rise: Among U.S. adults ages fifty and older, the divorce rate has roughly doubled since the 1990s.

It is time to rethink our approach. Most experts agree good parents must start by being good partners. And if you are a single parent, you also need to nourish outside relationships including friends, colleagues, and potential partners.

One blogger shared some valuable insight in a 2014 *HuffPost* article entitled "Why I Put My Husband Before Our Kids." Stephanie Jankowksi, who writes a blog titled *When Crazy Meets Exhaustion*, received lots of negative, emotionally charged feedback when she initially discussed the idea of putting her spouse first. She wrote a follow-up defending her position and wrapped the article with this:

"Valuing our spouses, loving our children, and finding time for ourselves can all coexist within a healthy marriage and happy family. When building anything, a strong foundation is crucial, which is why I continue to put my relationship with my husband before our kids. As **parents**, our goal for the future includes happy, healthy children who are independent of us, and maybe a beach house. As a **couple**, we hope to avoid staring blankly at one another from across the kitchen table, barely familiar with the person we married fifty+ years ago. And as a **woman**, I proudly wear the titles of Wife and Mom, but before I was married with the children, I was Stephanie, and I refuse to lose sight of myself."

We happen to agree. And single moms can also fall into the trap of putting their kids' needs ahead of their own. It's time to change the family hierarchy. Every person in the family is on equal footing; no one should have VIP or priority status. No one comes first, second, or twenty-ninth. Give up the martyr status. No one cares what you are sacrificing and no one else is going to award you for it. Quite the contrary, you may find yourself left behind by your peers in the end.

As we move into the next section, ponder this question:

If barred from any discussion about kids while out to dinner with your partner, would you be staring into your martini and wondering what was on Netflix?

Answer these questions honestly:

* When is the last time you shared a romantic date night, weekend, or vacation with your partner, just the two of you?
* How often do you feel disconnected or like you're just "rooming" with your spouse or partner?

Now write a plan to reconnect with your partner over the next 30 days. Include three things you can do to make your relationship a priority.

1.

2.

3.

"There comes a time when we have to let go of our children so that we can find the time to create balance in our life."

chapter four

HOW THE HELL DID I GET *HERE*?

Or: I'm definitely not in Kansas anymore...and why am I wearing these shoes?

Carly
This was never how she imagined approaching fifty would look: a financially successful wife, three college-educated kids, a beautiful home and all the money she could possibly need. To a casual observer, she lived the venerable ideal. But now Carly was searching for her identity from the inner sanctum of an in-patient treatment center. This wasn't part of the plan. After fifteen years of marriage and the revelation of her wife's infidelity, things fell apart. It wasn't that her union couldn't be salvaged; she had forgotten what her half of that union was all about. Who was she, separate from the others in her family?

Carly's predicament is actually a common one. It doesn't matter the circumstances that lead you to this place—a relationship crisis, the loss of a job, kids moving away, aging, or even simply boredom. Lots and lots of women have told us that one day they woke up to the realization that they have invested one hundred percent of themselves in developing other people's identities. They struggle to feel the joy and sense of purpose that comes with living a life that reflects their passions and skill set. And some have even forgotten how to have fun.

After months of therapy, Carly was able to see how she lost herself in the relationship. She had to do some work on herself before deciding whether to repair or end her partnership. First, she created a plan to nurture her own interests and passions and set some goals and boundaries. In time, Carly reconciled with her wife and is working on not letting the relationship swallow her identity. Carly is taking a management course, has joined a pickleball league, and is planning a trip with college friends. She said prioritizing her needs has made her relationship stronger and she knows nurturing her own passions will have a lasting impact.

Kayleigh
Kayleigh's transformation started with the loss of her brother in 2010. She realized that tomorrow is not guaranteed and she began to rethink her life choices and to focus on what truly made her happy. "I took up art because my job had changed and it wasn't what it used to be. I wasn't feeling passionate anymore and that was spilling over into my personal life."

Kayleigh didn't make a change immediately. She was making a larger salary than her husband and carrying the benefits for her family. She felt the financial burden of staying in her current job. She knew if she was going to leave her job it had to be "worth her while." After a year of searching for different options, there was a re-organization at her company and the new role she was offered was clearly not a good fit. Kayleigh met with her boss to discuss her future. After a year of reflection and job searching, her whole mindset had changed. She told her boss that she needed to put herself first, and that she was prioritizing her health and her happiness. "I knew things would work out. I thought I'd be a blubbering mess, but I was relieved. It was like a weight had been lifted off my shoulders."

The months that followed were glorious and Kayleigh says she has no regrets about the decision to leave her job. She had a severance package to fall back on while she was figuring out what she really wanted to do. And while her husband was a bit nervous, he was completely supportive of the move. She called this period of transition scary, knowing she had to make some financial adjustments and sacrifices, but also exciting. Her parents also backed her decision. Her dad called her on her last day in the job saying he wanted to wish her well and hoped she would find what makes her truly happy.

Fast forward a couple of years and Kayleigh says she now feels more connected to her heart. (That's where your Oz lives!) She said she is less stressed and happier, referencing this quote from Martin Luther King, Jr.: "You don't have to see the whole staircase, just take the first step." A few years ago, she felt trapped, unsettled and unsupported. Today she feels free to make decisions, have faith and be more present, to live in the moment.

Kayleigh is thriving. She took her passion for art and creativity and began a business refinishing and reselling furniture. First, she sold her products on Facebook and other online platforms. Today, she has a storefront in a small town in New Hampshire. She says she is happy because she is using her creativity and making a difference.

Kayleigh is on a journey to her version of Oz. She is clicking her heels and finding her way home. It's the place where what you do and what you value intersect.

"Clicking to me means there is happiness in all areas of my life. I love what I'm doing at work, my family life is good, I have down time, I have the time to take care of myself. I have an all-around balance in my life."

Jennifer

Jennifer is a forty-year-old mother of three. A trained nurse and accomplished pianist, she made the decision to stay home and raise her three children. "I wanted to be a stay-at-home mom. I knew I was really lucky to be able to afford to stay home and raise my kids." But somewhere over the last eleven years, she lost herself. She realized that her days consisted of cooking, cleaning, disciplining, and catering to her family's needs. Her "big day out" was attending a local Bible study every Thursday morning. By the time her children were eleven, nine, and five, she felt unsatisfied and bored with her life. She truly felt like her life had little meaning.

Jennifer knew she had to make a change so she decided to go out and get a job. The first place she applied was Lowe's home improvement store. Why Lowe's? Did Jennifer have an interest in home repair? Quite the contrary. "I thought the job would be flexible. I would be able to work around my children's schedules and still be home to cook dinner for my husband."

Was Jennifer's husband expecting that? Absolutely not. But somehow her first response was to put her talents, passions, and needs aside and take a job that would be unfulfilling. They didn't need the money. She was looking for a reason to get out of the house and meet new people. But instead of trying to find something that would enrich her life, she chose a job that would have as small an impact as possible on her family.

Jennifer's response is not uncommon. Instinctively, mothers often put their children's and/or partner's needs first. Jennifer has a supportive husband who is willing to step in at a moment's notice and make dinner, help with homework, or take the kids to the library. Her husband encouraged her to think outside the box and to look for a part-time job that would enhance her life rather than just fill the time.

With her husband's support and urging, Jennifer started looking for jobs through a different lens. She started looking for opportunities where she could be creative, develop a skill, and use her talents. Within a week, she was hired as an interim organist at a local church. "The first time I sat down to play it was as if this peace came over me. I was so happy to be playing music again. And then at the end of the service, they handed me a check for two hours' work. It was more money than I would have made working for a week at Lowe's!"

Jennifer found a way to connect to her talent and passion and was given an amazing opportunity. And guess what? Her family didn't suffer. Yes, they ate different food when dad was cooking and they went on different adventures but it was a great experience for everyone. The kids had quality time with dad, and she had time each week to nurture her gifts. Spending time doing something she truly loved—music—allowed her to be a more positive parent. And she realized that her children didn't need her as much as she thought they did. Everyone was absolutely fine when she took a little time for herself.

Like many of the women we talked to, there often comes a time when we have to let go of our children so that we can find the time to create balance in our life. The realities of parenting often take priority in our lives, leaving us with time for little else. But the day will come when you will parent yourself out of a job. And we are arguing that it's best to always be ready by keeping yourself challenged and relevant. When they leave, will

WAKING OZ

YOU be ready?

Here is another column written by co-author Sue Tabb about the realities of parenting:

My Painting

There is a painting I created some time ago that I really treasure. It's not perfect by any means, but it's mine. I chose the colors and executed each stroke and even its imperfections have a way of growing on you after a while. When you look up close, it's a series of attempts, mostly achieved by trial and error. And there are plenty of missteps that were the result of flawed judgment or a lack of skills, or both. But I learned quite a bit from each of those artistic shortcomings.

Here's the thing I love most though: When you stand back and look at this creation as the sum of its parts, as a composite work created from a unique perspective, it all comes together in a most remarkable way. Parenting is kind of like that. We produce distinctive masterpieces that are shaped by our influence. Glorious and unique and perfectly imperfect.

The difference is that I can keep my painting. My kids will leave. And they are nearly ready. My husband and I have put a lot of heart and soul into these works of art—we have given them color and texture and a framework to live within. But when are we ready?

Letting go of something so treasured and rare is difficult. It seems like just yesterday our daughters were begging us to read Where the Wild Things Are *in our best monster voice (Let the wild rumpus begin!) or pleading with us to hear* Love You Forever *for the 147th time. My youngest nearly clawed my chest to shreds, clinging to me in those first weeks of kindergarten. Blankie and Binky and Bunny came everywhere we went. And our American Girl dolls—Winnie and Molly—had a seat at the dinner table.*

We were a unit—the core four. And we traveled in a pack. We went to the park and apple picking and to the downtown festivals and out for ice cream. We went to the beach and to the mall and out for dinner. All for one and one for all. Mom, Dad, a girl with twinkling blue eyes and a blonde ponytail and another, only slightly smaller, with an infectious giggle and a stunning head of brunette curls.

Sure, there have been challenges and spirited discussions and the kind of disappointments that come with growing up. There have been false starts and teachable moments and tears. But through it all, we have held our two masterpieces tight. Owning them.

But the paintings are dry. They are ready to be shared with the rest of the world. Not everyone will recognize their value; but those who do will receive the greatest gift I can imagine giving to anyone. A priceless work of art with immeasurable worth. So when are we ready?

It seems that matters little. Time passes and kids yearn to break away, not because they love us any less but because they have the capacity to love even more. They are ready for new relationships and sticky breakups and challenges they've never imagined. They are ready to feed their minds and search for what makes their souls sing and to conquer the world with their own set of paints and brushes.

We aren't ready but they are. So I'm trying to take in the essence of this work so it stays with me always. It is a treasure like none other and although it is a difficult prospect, it is only right to share its beauty and let it bring joy to others. It is quirky and funny and smart and beautiful and has passion and heart like I've never seen. I can't wait to see who it touches and I can't wait to welcome it back home to where it will always have a place and be infinitely loved.

My painting.

So, the choice is all yours. We'll say it again. Kids grow up, plans get altered, marriages can change. Don't wait until the proverbial shit hits the fan to get moving. You need to decide now what your life will look like if and when it's you alone looking back in the mirror. Putting yourself out there is scary, making changes can be hard— but what is the alternative?

As we move into the next chapter, ponder this question:

How long are you going to drive the minivan?

* Answer these questions honestly:

* When was the last time you did something that truly spoke to your heart?

* How often do you do things for your family that they could do for themselves?

* What is one thing you would choose to do if you had more time?

Write about three things you can do to work toward achieving balance in your life:

1.

2.

3.

"Being in your element helps you to connect to what is fundamental to your purpose and well-being."

chapter five
IT'S NEVER TOO LATE FOR A DO-OVER

Or: Don't you want an impressive eulogy?

It's never too late for a do-over. But come on, if not now, when? Co-author Deirdre often asks the students in her first-year seminar class to complete a short essay assignment. They need to write a paragraph about how they hope people will describe them in thirty years. If your children were to describe you, what words would they use? One friend tells the story of when her five-year-old son had to write about what made his mom special and he wrote, "She cleans toilets, cooks dinner, and makes sure our house is spotless." Is that how you want your children to see you? Ask yourself some difficult questions:

* Do your children see you as someone who loves their job or complains about going to work each day?
* Do your children see you as someone who is joyful?
* Would your children describe your days as filled with creative endeavors or just killing time?

Children watch closely. They see how parents prioritize their time. It doesn't matter if you are a stay-at-home mom or you work full or part-time. When you are home, are you present? Are you happy with your lifestyle? Are you joyful?

When was the last time you did something you were really passionate about? Something that reflects who you are or what you value? Something that truly touched your heart?

In his book, *The Element,* Ken Robinson talks about how important it is to find your element, the place where passion, talent, and opportunity come together. According to Robinson, you can find your element in work, in school, or in a hobby. Finding your element is crucial to personal happiness. When people achieve their element, they feel truly connected to what is important and are ultimately inspired to achieve their greatest potential. Robinson describes the conditions that allow people to find their element. He draws on the stories of a wide range of people: cartoonist Matt Groening, choreographer Gillian Lynne, musician Paul McCartney, and Olympian gymnast Bart Conner to name a few.

Many people choose a career based on talent. You become a math teacher because you were good at math. You become a researcher because you got high marks in biology. You decide to teach third grade because people always told you that you were "good with kids." But is talent enough? Robinson would say no. According to Robinson, "The element is the meeting point between natural aptitude and personal passion."

As we grow older, we convince ourselves that our capacities decline, that opportunities we have missed are gone forever. Many people do not understand that they can find their element at any time in their life. Being in your element helps you connect to what is fundamental to your purpose and well-being. Just because you are good at something doesn't mean you have to keep doing it forever. Think about how you fill your days.

Do you feel truly passionate about what you do? Are you actually listening to your heart? Try this today:

1. Imagine that your life could be different. Would you live in the same community? Would you have the same job? How would you spend your free time?

2. Write down as many words as you can to describe what

you would really like to be doing. How would you describe a life that reflects your priorities, loves, and values? Be honest with yourself.

3. Think about one thing you could do this week to connect to your heart and bring you closer to those things.

Look, we all have a heart, but do you know what yours is saying? And if so, do you make the time to respond to it? It's important your family sees you doing things that truly touch your heart. Children who see parents finding time to make a difference will grow up to be adults who change lives. It's easy to get caught up in the day-to-day tasks of life. We all get sidetracked by the demands of managing a family, a household, and work commitments. How often do you find yourself saying, "I can help next year" or "I will make a donation next week" or even "I'd love to learn how to do that someday"? But next week and next year and someday never come. Most of us feel like we have no time. But the truth is we are all busy, but busy doing what? Remember that a *busy* life is not necessarily a *full* life. There is a critical difference.

Commit to making a change now. Do something that makes a difference TODAY. Model for your children a life that prioritizes putting people and causes that you care about first. Because, face it, the fact is you are not going to get less busy. As optimistic as you might be that your schedule will free up soon, it's a fantasy. In our uber-digital world of hyper connectedness, it is too easy to be available and ready to react to all things at all times.

Only do the things that truly matter to you. That seems simple, right? But how many of us find ourselves serving on committees, going to meetings, or driving to an event and grumbling all the way there? Is that the model behavior we want our children to see? Do we want our children to say, "My mother served on more committees than anyone, but she was never happy?" It's time to wave the white flag. Either live a life that is dictated by others or create some boundaries that allow you to actually be you. Our kids say it to us all the time: "Mom, you do you!" Yes, that's what we've all been missing, especially women, as we seem more prone to make it all about the kids every minute of every day. We have a self-imposed standard that we have to be on call for them 24/7. And here's a fact: Our children don't want or need us to focus solely on them. Both children and parents need space to be creative, to develop, to grow. Your relationship with your child will be stronger if you each develop your own interests.

Here's the thing: You need to give up something in order to gain some time to connect with your heart, because that's the core of who you are. And for most of us that can just be letting go of our desire to appear on top of it all. (No one is.) So why not redirect some of that energy into something that makes your heart sing?

Unfortunately, so many people we talk to can't remember what that is or don't know how to begin to tune in to that part of themselves again. We need to clear away some of the other noise in order to make room. We need to teach our children to clear away the noise. Show your children what it means to prioritize what truly speaks to your heart and act on it. Have honest conversations about what matters to them. Help them connect to their heart. It is possible. No more excuses.

And remember that if you truly listen to your heart and prioritize your commitments, you will find time you didn't think you had. Both authors have felt their lives were too busy to add another thing. Deirdre held down two jobs while helping her daughter Maggie start a non-profit theater program for underserved students in Lawrence, Massachusetts.

"The Performing Project," still thriving twelve years later, not only changed Deirdre's perspective, it changed the perspective of her entire family with respect to the best use of their time. Sue had a similar experience when she helped her daughters, who were concerned about feeding the hungry, launch a year-long project to raise money for local food shelters. The "Bread and Butter Project" provided help to others and a lot of inspiration to act in a way that reflects your values.

But starting a non-profit may not be your thing. And that's totally fine. Our point is to make room to do or chase something. You don't have to cure cancer or establish world peace (although that would be nice); you just need to find something that makes you feel engaged, inspired, and satisfied with how you are using your time and talents. That's the key to finding your Oz. That's the way "home." You have the power, but you have to click those heels. Maybe you've always wanted to travel to Ireland to see where your ancestors came from, or to tap into your creative side by learning how to paint, or to sing in a local choir. The thing is, if you aren't kicking up the bricks a bit, the yellow brick road will lead you nowhere fast. And don't you want to be heading somewhere?

We all have opportunities to connect to our heart. Sometimes we say no because we are too tired, we feel overwhelmed, we think we have nothing to offer. But we all have something to offer and we all need to feel like the way we live our life reflects what's important to us. What truly speaks to you? We are going to bet that a perfectly made bed isn't on the list. Let go of something. Life is short, and there are infinite possibilities for growth and new experiences. We'll say it again, look down—you are wearing the shoes. You have the power to make a change. If not now, when?

As we move into the next chapter, ponder this question:

Would you rather be spinning your wheels or driving the badass bus?

Answer these questions honestly:

* When was the last time you felt powerful or in control of your destiny? What were you doing during that time?

* Think about the people you admire. Have they reinvented themselves personally or professionally? Overcome challenges?

* How often do you start a sentence with the words "Someday" or "Eventually" or "When I have the time/money/freedom"?

Write down the biggest obstacle you can think of that gets in the way of you grabbing the wheel and taking charge of your future. What three things can you do right now to invalidate that excuse?

1.

2.

3.

"Change is scary, but don't let the fear of failure paralyze you."

chapter six

WANT TO PLAY WITH A LITTLE FIRE?

Or: Are you scared? Good!

Fire is good. It generates heat and light. And, yeah, sometimes you get burned. But you often have to be willing to step on some hot coals in order to get where you want to go. And there will be obstacles; remember the lions and tigers and bears? Well, it's something like that. In the end, playing with fire has risk but there is always risk in anything worth doing.

Making a change can be scary but staying still is so darn boring! And we all make excuses, reasons we couldn't possibly make a change because, let's be honest, staying still is safer. And these authors know all the excuses because we've used them too.

Excuse #1: "My kids need me." Reality check: Our kids don't need us as much as we think. They are much more resilient, resourceful, and self-sufficient than we give them credit for. We just don't always give them the opportunity to flex those muscles. They can probably find a ride home from lacrosse practice if you occasionally have a conflict. We bet they could piece together something to eat for dinner if you had a class to attend. They could even walk a half mile home from their friend's house if you had some work to do. Generations before us made out just fine. Why do we think our kids are so much more fragile?

Excuse #2: "I don't have the time." We all have the same amount of time every day. You have as much time as anyone; you need to decide if you are using it wisely. You may have a busy life, but are you living a full life? We bet there are plenty of things you do in the course of a day that are not as necessary as you may think. Many of us spend countless hours on the phone, watching Netflix, checking our Facebook accounts, or serving on committees that don't matter to us. Decide what you can cut so you can make time for things that make you feel happy and fulfilled.

> *"Don't say you don't have enough time. You have exactly the same number of hours per day that were given to Helen Keller, Louis Pasteur, Michelangelo, Mother Teresa, Leonardo da Vinci, Thomas Jefferson and Albert Einstein."*
> ~H. Jackson Brown, Jr.

Excuse #3: "I'm exhausted. I don't have the energy to add something to my life." Another reality check: when we do something we are truly passionate about, it actually energizes us. Have you ever had the feeling that the more you do, the more you can do? That's because doing things that make you feel accomplished, or challenge your brain, or move you toward a goal can infuse you with energy you didn't even know you had.

If I only had a brain. When was the last time you really used your brain? (Not to decide what to cook for dinner, or to schedule the next four-hour meeting at work, or to compare how many calories were in a power bar.) When was the last time you had a thought that truly energized you? When was the last time you really had to think?

Here's the unfortunate truth: many of us stop thinking about things that matter to us—the things that challenge our brains and drive our passions. It's not that we are unintelligent or uninformed; we just get consumed by everyday life and making sure that the other members of our family—mainly our kids—have what they need and are served well. While that is admirable, we often sacrifice more than we think. We end up thinking a lot about how to get through the day and are rarely left with the time or energy to nurture substantive thought. But kids grow up and leave. You may have twenty years ahead until retirement. What are you going to do? 7,300 days: how are you going to fill them?

Life begins at the end of your comfort zone. Many of us have gotten way too comfortable living in the shadows of our families. It is time to realize your personal growth and happiness are important too. And sometimes that means you have to move into a space that is unfamiliar and scary. Here are two personal stories about a time when we, the authors, stepped outside our comfort zones to learn new skills and challenge our brains. In the interest of full disclosure, it can be terrifying. But the energy you feel when you have met a challenge head-on is life changing.

Deirdre was an elementary school teacher for ten years when she decided to stay home with her son, Colin. Skip ahead four years and she had three children: Colin (age four), Erin (age two), and Maggie (six months). She loved her kids, but she was going crazy! She felt like the only reading material she had tackled started with "That Sam I am" and ended with "I do not like green eggs and ham!" She needed a challenge. When her friend Beth asked her to teach a class at a local community college, she was extremely apprehensive. "I don't teach college students," she said. After six months of repeated urging and reassurance from Beth that she'd be great at it, she said yes. She was terrified and unsure she had anything to offer her students. "Me, a college professor?" she thought. She had only fifteen weeks of information, a textbook, and a prayer.

So what did she do? Click: she dove right in. And what she found was that she actually knew quite a lot. She had a lot to share and her students were genuinely interested. But, more importantly, she had a lot to learn. Every week she spent reading journal articles, poring over her textbook, and reaching out to other colleagues. Every day she was challenged to learn something new. Suddenly, even with caring for three children under four, she had new-found energy. She was as excited to spend time with her children as she was to spend time with students. She didn't make a lot of money teaching that course, but she gained invaluable experience. Seven years later, she was hired as a full-time professor.

Sue was a major market radio personality for five years before leaving to raise her two young daughters. Like Deirdre, being home full time became frustrating because she felt like she wasn't challenging herself to learn anything new. After a year or so, she decided to take a job as a part-time newspaper reporter (with zero experience) for a little more than minimum wage. She was scared to death but excited to learn a new skill. She was no longer interviewing A-list celebrities but covering everyday people. It wasn't as glamorous for sure—in fact one day she was knee-deep in mud meeting Bucky the Goat while interviewing a local winemaker. Yup, it was a far cry from interviewing Ben Affleck just a year prior, but she was happy she did it. It was humbling, but it gave her a new skill set. Sue ended up launching a lifestyle column and earning a New England Press Association Award.

We all have opportunities to use our brain. Sometimes we say no because we think the money isn't worth it, we aren't sure we have the skill set, or we are just plain scared. But fear can be good. And we can tell you that using your brain will change your life. Challenge yourself to step outside your comfort zone and learn something new!

Here's why it's important to continually learn, grow, and develop your own interests: people lose their jobs, marriages break up, kids go on to college, careers, and living independently from you. The only thing that stays constant is your need to rely on yourself. You can maintain the status quo or you can choose to reinvent yourself and live your best life.

We like the quote by JP Morgan that says, "The first step towards getting somewhere is to decide that you are not going to stay where you are." True, but that takes a whole lot of courage. Which brings us back to the *Wizard of Oz*. Play with a little fire. Just light the match and be happy you're made of more than hay. And remember that even if you get the occasional burn, and we all do, you're wearing the shoes. Click!

Excuse #4: "What if I fail?" Fear is probably the most common excuse. Change is scary, but don't let the fear of failure paralyze you. Understand that moving out of your comfort zone can be unsettling but being scared is okay; it means you're moving forward. Surround yourself with people who will support your change; get advice from others; speak up and ask for what you need. It's hard to be vulnerable, but it's harder to look back with the "woulda-coulda-shoulda" kind of regret. Don't settle for a mediocre life.

As we move into the next chapter, ponder this question:

Would you rather risk playing with fire and getting burned or playing it safe and getting...nothing?

Answer these questions honestly:

* When is the last time you used your brain to learn a new skill?

* How often do you try something that makes you a little uncomfortable?

* What is the worst thing that can happen if you try something new? Is it an outcome that you can live with? If so, why not take the risk?

Write about one way you can challenge yourself to try something outside your comfort zone:

_____

"Failure is part of the journey; it is propelling you toward a bigger something."

chapter seven
ON FALLING DOWN SPECTACULARLY

Or: Expect to fail. That's part of the journey.

Failure is not always bad. If you learn from it, it breeds experience and something to draw from to become better. The failing is part of the journey; it is still propelling you toward a bigger something. You have to see each step as a piece of a much bigger picture or goal. You will have to use your failures to readjust the course so you can get to the final destination.

Several top colleges have begun to address the overwhelming problem that their students don't know how to fail. Suffering from years of helicopter parenting and competitions where everyone gets a trophy, students arrive at college paralyzed with a fear of failure. At Smith College, an initiative called Failing Well was created to destigmatize failure and strengthen student resilience. Freshmen enter a lecture hall and are greeted by a large screen projecting students and faculty members sharing their college failures. Administrators and professors work to change the misconception about failing, encouraging students to see it as a part of the learning experience. For many students at competitive colleges, failure can be unfamiliar and crippling. The goal is to diminish the fear of failure so students can take more risks.

And Smith is not alone in addressing this crisis around failure. Over a decade ago, faculty at Harvard and Stanford coined the term "failure deprived" to refer to students who appeared to be high achieving but were unable to cope with the minor setbacks in life.

We know that the incidences of anxiety and depression are rising on college campuses today. The demand for college counseling services is on the rise. Stanford started an initiative called the Resilience Project in an "attempt to normalize struggle." Soon other programs began emerging: The Success-Failure Project at Harvard, The Princeton Perspective Project, and Penn Faces at the University of Pennsylvania. Davidson College even created a failure fund, which gives students grant money to undertake projects where they are encouraged to fail.

And it's not just college students who are afraid to fail. Many of us spend our time paralyzed by fear of failure. And here's something to consider: No great success was ever accomplished without failure. Do you know it took Edison 10,000 attempts to create the light bulb? Edison is actually quoted as saying, "I've not failed. I've found 10,000 ways that didn't work." So how do you start to get past the fear of failure?

1. Come up with a "What If" scenario. What if I failed? What is the worst thing that could happen? Most of the time the fear of failure is a lot worse than the reality.

2. Imagine how your life could be different if you took this risk and succeeded. Visualize your success.

3. Set a timeline and stick to it. It's easy to say "I'll do it tomorrow," or "I'll do it next week." Risk is never going to be easy. Commit to doing one thing today that scares you.

4. Share your plan with someone who will help keep you accountable.

5. Realize that it may take you several tries to reach your goal. But rather than looking at those times as setbacks, look at them as periods for growth.

WAKING OZ

"Everything you want is on the other side of fear."
~ Jack Canfield

Many of us look at successful women and imagine that their path to success was easy. But many of the most successful women experienced failure after failure before finally achieving success. Here are two women who failed and then went on to click their heels. Their stories might surprise you.

Oprah Winfrey

After a childhood of abuse and neglect, Oprah Winfrey went to live with her father who encouraged her education. She received a scholarship to Tennessee State University where she majored in communications and interned at a local radio station. When she was eventually hired to work at a local television station, the producer fired her saying she was "unfit for television."

In 1983, Oprah relocated to Chicago and began hosting a talk show called AM Chicago. Within a few months, the show went from last to first in the ratings, beating out Donahue, which was the number one show at the time. The show was eventually renamed The Oprah Winfrey Show and syndicated across the country.

Arianna Huffington

Arianna Huffington, one of the most powerful businesswomen today, is no stranger to failure. Although her first book did fairly well, her second book was rejected by thirty-six publishers. But Arianna actually looks at failure as the key to success. In an interview with CNN she said, "You can recognize very often that out of these projects that may not have succeeded themselves, other successes are built." Huffington is currently the President and Editor-in-Chief of the Huffington Post and the author of thirteen books.

"Nobody tells you about failure...People always talk about winning, vision boards, getting what you want. People also don't talk about fear. It's always keeping fear at bay. Squelching it. Throwing it away. I've embraced fear and

failure as a part of my success. I understand that it's part of the grand continuum of life. I've been through it all. Breakups, heartache, and I've lost a parent already. So now I get it at this age, I get that that is it. That life literally is what you make it."
~ Actor Viola Davis, Vulture, 2014

As we move into the next chapter, ponder this:

The people who experience incredible success have first been willing to fail spectacularly. Are you willing to blow it in the name of progress? Can you handle falling flat on your face?

Answer these questions honestly:

* When is the last time you tried something and failed?
* Who is counting your missteps or "failures?" Who will judge you?

Now write down one thing you will do THIS WEEK that is risky but has a great payoff in the end whether you succeed or not:

_____

"Just because you haven't found the most fulfilling career by age forty, doesn't mean your life has to remain status quo."

chapter eight
WOMEN WHO ARE CLICKING

Or: These broads are kicking ass!

So, are you inspired to start clicking? So many women think it is too late to make a change in their career, again making decisions based on fear. Our society perpetuates the idea that success is achieved early in your career through hard work and determination. Just because you haven't found the most fulfilling career by age forty, doesn't mean your life has to remain status quo. Women in their forties and fifties often bring life experience and a different perspective to their work. If you want to be inspired by some amazing women who started clicking later in life, read on!

Laura Ingalls Wilder, who is noted for her *Little House on the Prairie* books, married as a teenager and spent most of her life helping her husband on his farm. She periodically wrote articles for the *St. Louis Star* but didn't publish her first book until age sixty-four. With the encouragement of her daughter Rose, Ingalls Wilder decided to write the Little House series based on her own life's events. Her last book in the series, *These Happy Golden Years*, was published when Ingalls Wilder was seventy-six.

Grandma Moses is a world-renowned American folk artist. She didn't begin painting until the age of seventy-six when she was unable to embroider due to arthritis. Art collector Louis Caldor discovered Grandma Moses' paintings while on vacation and recommended that they be included in a Museum of Modern Art exhibition. Grandma Moses continued to paint for twenty-five more years, creating over 1,000 paintings. Her paintings continue to grow in popularity, and now sell for over one million dollars.

Vera Wang is a perfect example of someone who decided to take her career in a completely different direction in her forties. Before becoming a world-renowned fashion designer, Wang was a journalist and competitive figure skater who was inducted into the U.S. Figure Skating Hall of Fame. She graduated from Sarah Lawrence College with a degree in history and began working for Vogue as a senior fashion editor. She worked at Vogue for fifteen years before a short stint at Ralph Lauren as an accessories design director. While planning her own wedding, she was frustrated with the lack of chic bridal options. She decided to take her career in a completely different direction and is now known throughout the world as a major fashion and bridal designer.

Kathryn Bigelow is one of America's most influential female directors, but she did not achieve success until the age of fifty-seven. Bigelow began gaining recognition when she directed the 2008 drama, The Hurt Locker, receiving an Academy Award for Best Picture and Best Director. Bigelow is one of the few successful women directors in the film industry and she is outspoken against gender discrimination, stating that women should be judged solely based on their work, not their gender.

Viola Davis is the first African-American actress to win an Emmy for Outstanding Lead Actress in a Drama series for her lead role in the ABC series *How to Get Away with Murder*. But the road to success was not easy for Davis. Although she worked on the stage for several years and took on smaller roles on television shows like *Law and Order*, it wasn't until she landed a role opposite Meryl Streep in the 2008 film *Doubt* that Viola Davis became a household name. She was forty-three years old.

Julia Child, one of America's most iconic chefs, didn't even learn to cook until she was thirty-six years old! In fact, Child planned to become a novelist. She graduated from Smith College and worked in advertising and government intelligence. After her husband was stationed at the U.S. embassy in Paris, she began to study French cooking at Le Cordon Bleu and adapt it to the American palate. She wrote her world-famous cookbook *Mastering the Art of French Cooking*, which was a best seller for five consecutive years. At forty years old, Child achieved worldwide fame on the television show *The French Chef*, which aired on WGBH and was syndicated to ninety-six stations.

As we move into the next chapter, ponder this:

What will you talk about at the next family gathering? Will you discuss the job you are unhappy in, or the way, at fifty, you just taught your first spin class, published an e-book or learned to belly dance? Who would you rather be listening to?

Answer these questions honestly:

* Which woman's story spoke to you? Why?
* What characteristics do women who are actively searching for their version of Oz share?

Think about where you see yourself in five years. What is one small thing you could do THIS WEEK toward achieving that goal?

_____

What is one larger thing you can do in the next thirty days?

_____

"This is your one-and-only life. You can choose to live it the way it unfolds or design your life the way you choose it to be."

chapter nine
SAYING IT OUT LOUD

Or: Hello? Is this thing on?

"One of my best moves is to surround myself with friends who, instead of asking, 'Why?' are quick to say, 'Why not?' That attitude is contagious."
~Oprah Winfrey

There's something to be said for writing things down—a list of things to do, a set of goals, a journal entry. Creating a paper trail doesn't just help you remember things; it makes you accountable. Something that is documented becomes something you feel responsible for, something that is real and attainable and that you can check off the list. We suggest you take it one step further. Say it OUT LOUD. Telling someone you want to take a class, write a book, start selling jewelry on Etsy, or take up kickboxing is the best way to take the first step in moving that item forward. You are making a verbal commitment and you are putting it out to the universe. How do you get started? We call it the THREE Ss.

1. **SPEAK IT**: It's like taking vows; you are making a statement about your intentions and sharing it with others.

2. **SHARE IT:** Depending on who you share it with, you are creating a support network to help in the process of achieving the goal. You are affirming your intentions and abilities to yourself.

3. **STEP OUT:** Begin to take action (bold and deliberate).

So that's a good first step, but then you have to get to the *doing* part. Yeah, that's a little bit more complicated, but here's the thing: as a parent, you've probably helped your kid apply to college, fight a nasty virus, establish credit, learn to drive, get over a break up, and navigate the challenges of puberty. And now you say you can't figure out how to set up a website for your home business, find time to take a pottery class, or gather the resources to chair the non-profit event that means so much to you? That's bullshit, frankly. If it was something for your child, your partner, or someone in your inner circle, you would figure it out. *You* are in your inner circle. You are the innermost person in your circle. Ignoring you is like having an apple without a core; how would it hold up? What's holding you up? What does your core need to get stronger? Paying attention to its current state is a good first step. You need to be honest with yourself. What are you longing for? Are you even paying attention?

This is your one-and-only life. You can choose to live it the way it unfolds or to design your life the way you choose it to be. It's called living on purpose. What is your purpose? What are the ideas that you've always thought about but never acted on? We all have them but we shelf them because we get caught up in the same old routine. We forget to have adventures. We seem to lose our ability to be spontaneous when we become adults and even more so when we are parents. Some of that is unavoidable, but some is most certainly self-imposed. What can you do to break from routine and create adventures? What makes you feel amazing when you're doing it? What do people always say you are good at?

I would rather be ashes than dust; I would rather that my spark should burn out in a brilliant blaze than it should be stifled by dry-rot; I would rather be in a superb meteor, every atom of me in a magnificent glow than in a sleepy and permanent planet; the proper function of man is to live, not to exist; I shall not waste my days in trying to prolong them; I shall use my time.
~ Jack London

The key is to take yourself by surprise. This can be as easy as buying a vegetable you've never tried at the grocery store to planning your dream trip to Greece. It could be writing a letter to your significant other or wearing rhinestone-studded glasses. Maybe you'll read Moby Dick for the first time. Maybe you'll learn how to play the guitar. Maybe you'll take a public speaking course or learn to speak Spanish. Maybe you'll move like lightning toward something or maybe you'll start at a slow crawl. Everyone's approach will be different. Everyone's speed will be different. And everyone's end goal will be a moving target that is constantly evolving. Therein lies the beauty of OZ. It is not a defined place or thing. It is simply our version of a fulfilling life.

As we move into the next chapter, ponder this:

Are you living your life with purpose? If not, what are you waiting for? LOOK DOWN and remember: you're always wearing the shoes. Click!

Answer these questions honestly:

* When is the last time you wrote down your personal and professional goals? Are they different today from twenty years ago? Are there common themes?

* When is the last time you talked about them? To whom?

"We need to stop seeing ourselves as the center of our children's universe. We are the center of our own universe."

KICK UP A TWISTER, SISTER!

Or: Strapping on Your Ruby Red Shitkickers

"It's easy to come up with big ideas. Just think of something that everyone agrees would be 'wonderful' if it were only 'possible'—and then set out to make it possible."
~Armand Hammer

Here it is! We've come to the point in this journey when you have to put your money where your mouth is. It's time to come up with a real plan to create a more purposeful, fun, fulfilling life that reflects who you are. This is the time when we ask that you reflect, write, declare, and make actionable plans. We hope you feel ready to author your own story and add some really juicy chapters. We are here to help.

Whether you want to pursue a hobby, start a business, do more charitable work, or travel to a locale on your bucket list, right now is a good time. It doesn't matter if you have toddlers or teens, you need to make yourself a priority and build in time to feed your interests and passions. Decide that your commitment to growing is bigger than your commitment to staying the same.

You've already taken the first step. You took the time to read this book in an effort to do something for YOU. Congratulations for recognizing that continual growth and change is good. Kudos for listening to your inner drive and trusting your gut. Be bold enough to look the world straight in the face and decide you will be open to having new experiences or rekindling old passions that you abandoned long ago. Your kids will benefit from seeing you take a more active approach to your life. You are not doing them a disservice when you invest in your own passions. We need to stop seeing ourselves as the center of their universe. We are the center of our own universe.

So, it's time to kick up a twister, sister.

We dubbed it "The Twister Effect," meaning you intentionally create a whirlwind of disorder and chaos in order to promote growth or positive change. It is a deliberate attempt to kick up the dust, even if you're not sure how things will turn out. It's giving yourself permission to jump in puddles and to get muddy and to not make excuses for it, even when the outcome is not what was desired. This type of deliberate disorder has PURPOSE. How?

* Removing the stigma that surrounds this type of "messy living" gives us permission and courage to explore the unknown in a no judgment zone.

* When we try new things and create new circumstances, we build confidence and courage.

* We discover that it's okay to SUCK at something. We might suck at first and get better, or we might just suck period. Either way, we tried it. We moved out of our comfort zone and challenged ourselves. That's growth whether you succeed or fail.

* It encourages fun. We all need to have more fun and adventure in our lives. Strap on your reddest shoes and kick it up. Hard. Fun is a key ingredient in living fully.

* It promotes authenticity. We can accept our imperfections, embrace our newfound skills, or just laugh at the opportunity to fall down or fail with some serious flair. The more we share our experiences with others, the more real they will be.

* The movement created is always good; it propels you forward. Sure, if we're being real, you may feel like you are going in circles at times but there is a path being cut through and it's moving you in a new direction. So, what exactly is the EFFECT?

- Life gets messy BUT EXCITING
- Life gets scary BUT CHALLENGING
- Life gets unpredictable but INVIGORATING
- Life gets complicated but MEANINGFUL

We challenge you to get in there and move to the center where you can see the possibilities around you. Seeing it is the first step. Believing you can and should take advantage of it is the second. The third is the toughest—that's when you decide to actually make the leap, absolutely no excuses. The kids don't need you every minute, you do have enough time, you can budget the money, you can learn something new, you are smart enough, strong enough, and capable enough. No. More. Excuses.

Your future happiness is at stake here. No one else is responsible for how your life looks and feels. You can be a kick ass mom AND other things not related—a great painter, a businessperson, a gardener, a cook, a writer, a dancer, a philanthropist, a spiritual leader, a stand-up comic. You don't have to be, nor should you be, wholly defined by motherhood. This is the day that it can begin to change. It's not a quick fix, mind you, it's a process. But beginning is the only way to get there.

Now let's get more concrete. We've created a program to help you get started on your journey to Oz. Here's how it works: We've outlined nine core identifiers that will help you "identify" what values are most important to you. Some will resonate with you while others may not, depending on your individual skills, preferences, and goals. We suggest that you choose THREE that are in line with your personality. Once you choose what we refer to as your POWER 3, we ask you to devote THREE WEEKS to each to begin to kick up the dust (the Twister Effect!) and create some disruption. Those actions will begin to propel you toward your version of Oz—that place where *what* you spend your time doing actually reflects *who* you are. In the end, your activities should be a clear indicator of what you value and find satisfying in life.

Core Identifier One: The Learner

Learners love to discover; they are energized by gaining knowledge. Facts are fun! They love to read, research, and discuss what they are learning with others. They believe the process of learning is more important than being seen as an expert. Many subjects interest the learner so they engage in many different adult learning experiences. They thrive when they feel challenged and when they are asked to master a new content area or skill. In their view, each new experience is an opportunity for growth.

Some Ideas for The Learner

* Take a class on a subject that intrigues you like wine tasting, cake decorating, knitting, acting, coding, genealogy, gardening, etc.
* Attend a lecture
* Join a book club
* Learn a second language
* Read one of the great works of literature
* Go back to school to further your degree or earn additional credentials

If your core values include knowledge/learning/growth, you might set the following goals

* Week one: Attend a lecture
* Week two: Join a book club
* Week three and future goal: Go back to school to further your degree or earn additional credentials

Core Identifier Two: The Catalyst

Simply put, the Catalyst is someone who gets things rolling. She is the person who uses all her available resources to get things done...somehow, some way. Even when faced with obstacles or challenges, the Catalyst figures a way around to achieve the desired result.

The Catalyst believes only action can make things happen. Only action leads to performance. Once a decision is made, you cannot NOT act. This person learns more from doing than by discussion or theory. She seeks real experiences. A Catalyst can create momentum by leveraging their resources and influence.

A warning here to Catalysts, as these authors fall into the category. Some people who don't possess this personality trait may be intimidated by your "enthusiasm." (They may be the ones rolling their eyes when you announce your next greatest idea). It's important to understand that the comfort level YOU have with making a decision and acting on that decision is not shared by everyone. Your process may be a bit messier and more intuitive at times. Be sure to recognize the different approaches that others may bring to the journey. In more blatant terms: not everyone's red shoes work in quite the same way. They all have the power to get you where you are going but the path will be different for everyone. It is important to be self-aware and respectful of differences.

Some Ideas for The Catalyst

* Take the classes you need to finish a degree or certification
* Ask for a raise or apply for a new position
* Write a paper or article about your area of expertise
* Apply for an award or have someone nominate you for an honor you are deserving of
* Chair a board or sit on a committee
* Prepare a presentation, Ted Talk, or lecture on a topic of interest
* Mentor someone in your field

* Update your resume or bio

* Write articles for a publication, start a blog, or create a Facebook group on an area of interest

* Use LinkedIn or other professional sites to connect with people of influence

If your core values include achievement/recognition/success, you might set the following goals:

* Week one: Use LinkedIn to connect to people

* Week two: Write a paper or article about your area of expertise

* Week three and future goal: Take the classes you need to finish a degree or certification

Core Identifier Three: The Adventurer

The Adventurer simply seeks out new and exciting experiences. This person is not afraid to take a risk and charter unknown territory. She is the one who has the bucket list of places she wants to visit and things she wants to do. She is always planning the next trip or creating the itinerary for a group trip. Some books the adventurer may be interested in include:

* *1,000 Places to See Before You Die* by Patricia Shultz

* *50 States, 5,000 Ideas: Where to Go, When to Go, What to See, What to Do* by National Geographic and Joe Yogers

* *The Bucket List Book: 500 Things You Really Could Do* by Elise de Rijck

* Anything by Rick Steves

Keep in mind that the Adventurer does not have to be independently wealthy or living off of a family trust fund. There are lots of ways to have new experiences that won't leave you broke or in debt: you can create a travel fund and save for a big trip, you can search out deals on regional travel, you can uncover the hidden treasures around you locally, or even take a road trip with no particular destination. The point is not the cost of the trip or the magnitude of the destination, it is the quality of the experience. Did you do something for the first time? Did you have fun? Did you enjoy the people or culture? Did you strengthen a relationship? Did you relax and live in the moment? That's what adventure is all about.

Some Ideas for The Adventurer

* Plan your dream trip and pay for it in advance so there is no financial regret when you return

* Open a map and take a road trip to a nearby attraction and see where the day leads

* Find a local place to zipline, ride in a hot air balloon, parasail, kayak, etc.

* Choose to spend a night in a state you've never visited

* Visit a restaurant from "Diners, Drive-ins and Dives" and

get to know some of the "regulars"

* Do something that reminds you of being a kid—ride a bike, go bowling, rollerblade, visit an arcade, or play mini golf

If your core values include adventure/travel/play, you might set the following goals:

* Week one: Take a walk in a park you have never visited

* Week two: Plan a day trip out of state to explore a national park or historic landmark

* Week three and future goal: Set up a vacation fund. Put aside a certain amount every week and begin planning a vacation twelve months from today

Core Identifier Four: The Peacekeeper

Peacekeepers lead by supporting others. They are people who seek to feel centered and believe in harmony at all costs. The welfare of others is extremely important to them. Peacekeepers work to create balance in their lives and the lives of others.

Some ideas for The Peacekeeper

* Attend an interfaith service or a service from an unfamiliar denomination
* Take up meditation
* Attend a peace rally
* Keep a gratitude journal
* Walk a labyrinth
* Read a great work and reflect on its meaning
* Forgive someone
* Write a thank you note to a friend just to let them know how much you value their friendship

If your core values include faith/spirituality/peace, you might set the following goals:

* Week one: Write a thank you note
* Week two: Read a great work and reflect on its meaning
* Week three and future goal: Keep a gratitude journal. At the end of the year, reflect on what you are truly grateful for.

Core Identifier Five: The Integrator

The Integrator lives by the motto "The more, the merrier." They love to find opportunities for people to connect. People who are Integrators want to make others feel a part of the group. To them, everything is about making the circle wider; there is always room for another chair at the table.

Integrators see every interaction as an opportunity for connection. They love the energy of meeting new people and finding ways to help people connect.

Some ideas for The Integrator
- Create a family bucket list
- Plan a family reunion
- Reconnect with a friend from childhood
- Make amends with an estranged family member
- Plan a women's weekend away
- Make thoughtful homemade holiday gifts for family and/or friends
- Assemble a family cookbook with everyone's favorites recipes

If your core values include family/friendships, you might set the following goals:
- Week one: Create a family bucket list
- Week two: Reconnect with a friend from childhood
- Week three and future goal: Plan a family reunion

Core Identifier Six: The Enhancer

The Enhancer likes to leverage their time and money to maximize the yield. They Enhancer is the one who is always dreaming up a new business, side hustle, or way to have their money work smarter. This is the person who will always know when there is an early bird special at your favorite restaurant and have a Groupon for paint night with the girls. The Enhancer is not cheap nor is she greedy. She is frugal and forward thinking. She knows the value of money and time. She is someone these authors need to spend a LOT more time with! Everyone needs an Enhancer in their life. If it's not you, you can still listen and learn from one. Each of us can employ one or more of these ideas to maximize our resources. Good luck!

Some ideas for The Enhancer

* Take a money management class and plan dinner or drinks afterward as a reward for time well spent
* Start a vacation fund
* Moonlight doing something you love—drive for Uber, work as a food server, teach piano, get your real estate license, become a SAT tutor, etc.
* Buy a second house, cottage, or piece of land as an investment
* Purchase stock and/or learn more about the stock market
* Hire a financial planner

If your core values include financial security/wealth, you might set the following goals:

* Week one: Start a vacation fund
* Week two: Hire a financial planner
* Week three and future goal: Purchase stock and/or learn more about the stock market

Core Identifier Seven: The Rejuvenator

The Rejuvenator is in a continual search for *better*; better mental or physical health, better work/life balance, better sleep habits, or a better overall quality of life. The Rejuvenator isn't necessarily the person who spends two hours at the gym every day (it's painful to even write that), they are the person who is looking to continually challenge themselves with process improvement techniques. They keep life interesting and healthy and are always looking for inspiration from others to do so. The rejuvenator understands the importance of self-care but sometimes has to be reminded to practice it. She is often looking for someone to share in her experiences so that the journey is more enjoyable.

Some ideas for The Rejuvenator
* Take a yoga class/practice meditation
* Discover a new type of exercise—spin, kickboxing, yoga, rock climbing
* Bring your exercise routine outdoors—hiking, biking, water sports, etc.
* Try one new healthy food a week for ten weeks
* Sign up for a cooking class to learn how to prepare healthier meals
* Join a fruit and vegetable co-op
* Limit technology one hour before bedtime—this can lead to better sleep habits (go to bed earlier, let yourself wind down, etc.)
* Sign up for a 5K road race and train for it

If your core values include health/physical well-being, you might set the following goals:
* Week one: Limit technology one hour before bedtime
* Week two: Try one new healthy food a week for ten weeks
* Week three and future goal: Sign up for a 5K road race

Core Identifier Eight: The Romantic

The Romantic expresses love and devotion in a way that is intentional, unmistakable, and deeply affectionate. The Romantic loves dramatic and passionate gestures. The Romantic takes the time in both large and small ways to show people they love them. The Romantic works to strengthen intimacy in her relationships and often works hard to encourage the same actions from her partner or spouse.

Some ideas for The Romantic

- Plan a weekly date night
- Write a letter to your partner telling them how much they mean to you
- Plan a weekend away at a bed and breakfast you've never been to
- Buy some pretty lingerie
- Hold hands
- Watch a show together—all the episodes, all the seasons, together
- Make a music playlist that reminds you of your partner
- Make a digital photo album of a trip or trips you took together
- Make more time for sex
- Take a day off together and get in the car and just go. See where the day takes you.

If your core values include love/intimacy, you might set the following goals:

- Week one: Hold hands
- Week two: Plan a weekly date night
- Week three and future goal: Plan a weekend away at a bed and breakfast you've never been to

Core Identifier Nine: The Nurturer

A Nurturer works to help support people. They are energized by doing for others. They spend the majority of their time thinking about how to make a difference in the world. Nurturers offer support and encouragement while often helping people meet their basic needs. Nurturers feel fulfilled when they are connecting with people most in need.

Some ideas for The Nurturer

* Volunteer at a soup kitchen, food pantry, charity walk, or fundraiser.
* Commit a certain percentage—no matter how big or small—of earnings each year to charitable causes
* Offer to help a friend do something difficult—studying for a big exam, planning a wedding or funeral, moving
* Invite a homeless person to lunch
* Give an anonymous donation
* Donate unwanted or unused items to a local charity or thrift store
* Start a non-profit or a foundation for a cause you are deeply passionate about

If your core values include helping others, you might set the following goals:

* Week one: Clean out a closet and donate unwanted clothing to a charity
* Week two: Sign up to volunteer to serve at a soup kitchen
* Week three and future goal: Research nonprofits in your area and choose to volunteer at their annual fundraiser

POWER 3 WORKSHEET

CORE IDENTIFIER #1 _____

Week ONE goals	Status	Notes

Week TWO goals	Status	Notes

Week THREE goals	Status	Notes

Overall reflections and thoughts:

_____
_____
_____

Will you commit to continuing this progress? How?

_____
_____
_____

POWER 3 WORKSHEET

CORE IDENTIFIER #2 _____

Week ONE goals	Status	Notes

Week TWO goals	Status	Notes

Week THREE goals	Status	Notes

Overall reflections and thoughts:

_____

_____

_____

Will you commit to continuing this progress? How?

_____

_____

_____

POWER 3 WORKSHEET

CORE IDENTIFIER #3 _____

Week ONE goals	Status	Notes

Week TWO goals	Status	Notes

Week THREE goals	Status	Notes

Overall reflections and thoughts:

_____

_____

_____

Will you commit to continuing this progress? How?

_____

_____

_____

NOW, RELEASE THE FLYING MONKEYS!

Just remember you don't have to take a giant leap to make a change. Think about small changes that will have a big impact.

Setting small, measurable goals will give you the momentum you need to move forward. Remember, this is **all about you**. It is hard to commit to making your personal happiness a priority, but if you are feeling fulfilled you can be more fully present for others.

How does it feel to have spent just a few hours focusing on you? It probably felt pretty damn good, right? We're hopeful this book made you reflect on your life, reassess your options, and perhaps motivate you to dig down and tap into those interests and passions that may have been dormant far too long. You are worth your time. You are worth your energy. You are worth having a life that reflects all that is uniquely you. It's time to begin WAKING OZ.

Some thoughts to take away:

* It takes brains, heart, and courage to move forward—every little step counts. But don't be afraid to take the occasional giant leap. Trust your gut.

* Adventures can take many shapes and forms. Remember, your OZ is different than anyone else's. The yellow brick road has infinite pathways.

* Playing with fire is fun, but expect to get burned now and again. Missteps are just part of the crazy journey. Don't let the flying monkeys get in the way.

* It's never too late to start clicking your heels. You have one life; squeeze all the juice out of it you can. Let go of the idea that you have to focus solely on your kids—they have their own red slippers.

* You always had the power my dear and now is the perfect time. There is no great and powerful OZ. It was just you all along.

Now strap on those red shoes and kick some ass!

ABOUT THE AUTHORS

SUE TABB is a Gracie Award-winning broadcaster, public speaker, media expert and Boston morning radio show host. Sue works with a variety of charitable organizations with a special interest in those that support breast cancer patients and survivors. Sue has received a New England Press Association Award for her work as a humor columnist and loves to write on a variety of lifestyle topics. Sue is a graduate of Smith College and the mom of two fierce young women, Katie and Emma. She currently lives in Newburyport, MA with her husband, Tom, who encouraged her to realize her dream of becoming a published author.

DEIRDRE DUGGAN BUDZYNA is a professor of early childhood education and psychology, a theater director and producer and an educational coach. She lectures nationally on the topics of Multiple Intelligences in the Classroom, Creative Arts in Learning and Play Based Curriculum. Deirdre graduated from Mount Holyoke College and Lesley University and is the proud mother of three strong young adults: Colin, Erin and Maggie. She lives in Newburyport with her incredibly patient husband John.

Printed in the USA
CPSIA information can be obtained
at www.ICGtesting.com
LVHW022120221124
797277LV00004B/952